# Basic Financial Steps
*"That teaches you how to make your money work for you"*

Reginald Campbell

The Strategy Group—Greer, SC
ISBN: 979-8-9867069-0-0
Library of Congress Control Number: 2022914573
Title: *Basic Financial Steps: That teaches you how to make your money work for you*
Author: Reginald Campbell
Digital distribution | 2022
Paperback | 2022

ID 738004 © Laurie Barr - Art

# Forward

Reginald Campbell has a unique talent of managing finances and money. I've observed many that have benefited from his financial fitness instructions and guidance. I personally can endorse his teachings and applied principles that have placed me in a better financial position. These life changing principles and practices if applied, will teach you how to be disciplined and thoughtful of how you spend or invest your money. Most importantly, what I have learned is that it is not how much money you earn but how disciplined you with what you earn.


Regina D. Campbell, Ph.D.

# Reginald Campbell

Reginald I. Campbell is a gifted orator and facilitator in the area of spiritual development and practical living from all aspects of life. He is a talent with astonishing knowledge of finances and wealth management. As senior pastor of the House of Reconciliation, he possesses great administrative and leadership skills. As a result of his appointment to senior pastor by the founder, the late Dr. Sallie L. Campbell, membership has grown to an all-time high. He is the founders and president of The Campbell Foundation, a non-profit organization.

Reginald Campbell had over 20 years of experience in the corporate arena in which he has served in various positions such as Market Analyst and Marketing Executive for New Products and Trend Analysis. He currently is the President and CEO of The Strategy Group, LLC in which he is a Strategist and Technology Developer for international companies and corporations. He holds both a Bachelors and Master of Science in Business Administration.

He and wife Regina reside in Greenville, South Carolina. He has three children: Pharez, Elizabeth and Brandi.

# Acknowledgements

I appreciate and want to thank my loving and caring wife Regina D. Campbell, Ph.D. for assisting me in turning an idea into a vision that has now became a reality. Putting forth my first book will allow me to help and guide others in the best practices of basic financial principles.

This project is in honor of my late grandmother Dr. Sallie L. Campbell, who wrote many books and letters that were never published. This is in honor of what she exposed me to and inspired me to become, an author and an entrepreneur.

I would also like to thank Jeff Acker of Jeff Acker films for his hard work and years of collaborations with me on multiple projects.

To my loving children Pharez (Relicia), Elizabeth and Brandi and to my wonder grandchildren Alannah and Ayden thanks for your support.

To Charles Beasley, thanks for your tireless effort and unwavering support.

To all the House of Reconciliation friends, the Chat about life (Think Tank), and the Successful Living radio broadcast family, thank you all for your efforts and support in the publication of this book.

Finally, to all my friends and family thank you so much for your support.

# Table of Content

# Introduction

Successful Living was birthed by Reginald Campbell through his weekly radio program. The radio program focuses on issues that impact people's lives. Topics range from financial literacy to political insight to health and life benefits. Reginald Campbell teaches you how to live a balanced life to its fullest. He assists you in preparing for your future by applying discipline and processes that will lead to living a successful life in every area of your life (mind-body-spirit). You can hear Reginald Campbell's radio show on **spreaker.com** by going to the website or downloading the app for your mobile device.

In addition Reginald Campbell facilitates a "Chat about Life" small group session meeting monthly at a local library. "Chat about Life" is for individuals who seek practical advice for everyday challenges and problems.

# Chapter I
## What is Money?

*Money* is a substance used as a medium of exchange, measure of wealth, or means of payment

**Purpose of money** - Money is for the purpose of eliminating financial burden or should be used to advance your financial position. The list as follows:

*Pay down* – to acquire/purchase an item for the future.

*Pay off* – to eliminate a debt such off paying off a car note.

*Pay forward* – to pay ahead by 1 or more payments on a bill or item. For example you can double your car note payment which would put you ahead by 1 payment. This is a good idea when you have the ability to do so which will give you cushion or position in the case you encounter unforeseen financial challenges.

*Savings – to put money aside for a particular purpose*

*Emergency fund* –  to put money aside for unforeseen financial crisis

*Slush fund* – to do something that you didn't have budgeted or fund…

*Discretionary income* –  to have money left after paying monthly operating cost (bills). Use for personal use such as purchasing products or enjoying an evening out.  The key is to set a budget and utilize discipline and self-control.  It is always a good idea to carry money over from each pay check to build up your discretionary income.

*Investment* – is the process of which you put money into a system or something for the purpose of receiving a future gain that will better position your future. For example the purpose of obtaining a college degree is to be positioned where you can earned an income that will better position you for your future therefore paying for college is consider an investment because of its potential future earnings.

Types of Investments:

*Investment Portfolio* – a series of investments in a wide range of funds, companies, or bonds that allows the investor to diversify their portfolio to mitigate risk and increase the potential for financial gains
*401k* – to prepare for retirement

*Education* – to obtain a higher education degree

*College fund* – to invest money as to prepare for children to attend college, this should be started within the child's 1st year of age

*529 Plan* – a tax-free college savings plan that family and friends can contribute to that grows over time based on the investment options chosen

# *Assignment*

1. What are your thoughts towards money?

_____

_____

_____

_____

_____

2. Do you have a tendency to pay off bills or debt? If so, what bills or debt have you paid off?

_____

_____

_____

_____

_____

3. Do you currently have a savings account? Yes or No

4. How much on average do you save each month? (If no on the previous question) N/A
a. 25.00
b. 50.00
c. 75.00
d. 100 or above

5. Do you have any investment? Yes or No

6. What are your investments?

_____

_____

_____

_____

7. How much discretionary income do you have at the end of each pay period or month?
a. none
b. 25.00
c. 50.00
d. 75.00
e. 100 or above

# Chapter II

**Understanding of Money** – it is crucial that you understand your money and how to effectively manage what you earn. Money must be viewed as a commodity that is to be handled wisely.

*How to manage it* – the most important thing you can do with money is manage it. To do desire to earn more money is a good goal but it's crucial that you learn the ability and discipline on how to manage your earnings. To obtain more money is not always the answer but you need the wisdom and knowledge to manage your money. You should know where your money is being spent.

**Essential Financial Tools** – methods to assist you in managing your money

**Credit** – your financial position and viability

**What is a credit score/report** – measures your credit in a report that displays all activity concerning your loans, credit inquiries, and payment history. Your credit score is considered your FICO score (Fair Isaac Corporation) appendix A.

**How your FICO score is calculated** – according to myFICO score your FICO score is calculated from many different pieces of credit data in your credit report. This data is grouped into five categories 10% credit mix, 10% new credit, 15% length of credit history, 30% amount owed and 35% payment history. FICO scores can be both negative and positive in your FICO report. Making late payments can lower your FICO scores and making payments on time can re-establish a positive FICO score.

**Why should you have your credit monitored** – to make certain that the activity on your account are correct and that nothing has been charged to any of my accounts erroneously.

# Chapter III
## Budget

Everyone should have a budget. Budgets are not for those at a certain level of income but budgets are for the wealthy, middles class and everyone.

**What is a budget?** – a plan that captures your financial obligations, expenditures and income. A budget tracks your expenditures and is used to verify your purchasing power.

**How do I create one?** - list all of your expenditures to know exactly where you are spending your money, then list all sources of income. Listing these items gives you a clear picture of your monthly cash flow. Also it shows you your financials state.

**How should the budget be used?** – the budget should be used to verify affordability of potential purchases and opportunities, where you can cut or control expenditures.

# *Assignments:*

1. Do you know your credit score? Yes or No

2. What is your credit score or do you have a copy of your credit report? If you do not know here are several site you can obtain your credit score and report.

www.annualcreditreport.com

www.freecreditreport.com

www.creditkarma.com

3. Create a Budget (put on this page in the workbook) also provide a place where people can good obtain work sheet.

4. List your priorities: Monthly or One time purchase

_____
_____
_____
_____
_____
_____
_____

5. List your priorities that you can research and save money to purchase cash or pay a large payment when purchase to make your pay off less than a year.

_____

_____

_____

_____

6. Create a Budget using this budget worksheet

| Family Budget Worksheet | | | |
|---|---|---|---|
| **Income** | **Budget** | **Actual** | **Difference** |
| Salary/wages | | | |
| Salary/wages | | | |
| | | | |
| | | | |
| | | | |
| **Total Income** | | | |
| **Deductions** | **Budget** | **Actual** | **Difference** |
| Tithes/offerings | | | |
| Savings (to set aside) | | | |
| Child Support, Alimony, etc, | | | |
| 401k | | | |
| IRA | | | |
| Donations | | | |
| Pocket Money | | | |
| Other | | | |
| **Total** | | | |

| Housing | Budget | Actual | Difference |
|---|---|---|---|
| Rent or Mortgage Payment | | | |
| Home Insurance & Taxes | | | |
| Home Repairs (to set aside) | | | |
| Utilities | | | |
| Phone - Home | | | |
| Phone - Cell | | | |
| Cable | | | |
| Water Bill | | | |
| Gas | | | |
| Electric Bill | | | |
| Furniture | | | |
| Other | | | |
| Other | | | |
| **Total** | | | |

| Debt Payment | Budget | Actual | Difference |
|---|---|---|---|
| Credit Card Payments | | | |
| Student Loan Payments | | | |
| Other | | | |
| Other | | | |
| Other | | | |
| **Total** | | | |
| **Food** | **Budget** | **Actual** | **Difference** |
| Groceries | | | |
| Eating Out | | | |
| Coffee & Bar | | | |
| Dining Out | | | |
| Lunch | | | |
| Other | | | |
| **Total** | | | |

| Transportation | Budget | Actual | Difference |
|---|---|---|---|
| Car Payment | | | |
| Car Insurance + Taxes | | | |
| Car Maintenance (to set aside) | | | |
| Gas | | | |
| Public Transit, Parking, Tolls | | | |
| Other | | | |
| **Total** | | | |
| **Family** | **Budget** | **Actual** | **Difference** |
| Day Care & Babysitting | | | |
| Activities & Lessons | | | |
| Allowances & Child Support | | | |
| Family Entertainment | | | |
| Memberships | | | |
| Events | | | |
| Music | | | |
| Other | | | |
| Other | | | |
| **Total** | | | |

| Personal & Health | Budget | Actual | Difference |
|---|---|---|---|
| Clothing | | | |
| Toiletries & Care Products | | | |
| Haircuts | | | |
| Gym & Sports Club Memberships | | | |
| Health, Life, & Disability Insurance | | | |
| Vision/Contacts | | | |
| Doctor & Dentist Visits | | | |
| Prescription & OTC Drugs | | | |
| Other | | | |
| **Total** | | | |
| **Education** | **Budget** | **Actual** | **Difference** |
| Tuition | | | |
| Books & Fees | | | |
| Supplies | | | |
| Other | | | |
| **Total** | | | |

| Entertainment | Budget | Actual | Difference |
|---|---|---|---|
| Tickets for Shows & Games | | | |
| Books & Magazine Subscriptions | | | |
| DVDs, CDs, Video Games | | | |
| Other | | | |
| **Total** | | | |
| **Miscellaneous** | **Budget** | **Actual** | **Difference** |
| Charity, Gifts, & Offerings | | | |
| Pet Supplies & Vet | | | |
| Entertaining Guests | | | |
| Pocket Money | | | |
| Other | | | |
| **Total** | | | |
| **Summary Calculation** | | | |
| Total Expenses | | | |
| | | | |
| Remaining Funds | | | |

# Chapter IV
Purchases and Acquisitions

*Assets* - items that are purchased or accumulated that provide or hold a value for the owner; provides opportunity for advancement (ex. investment property, education, collectibles)

*Liabilities* - items acquired that do not hold financial value or cannot be used to help advance an individual (ex. jewelry, clothes, TVs)

# Assignment

1. List your assets

_____

_____

_____

_____

2. List your liabilities

_____

_____

_____

_____

3. Which of the items below can be considered an asset or liability?
Boat
Car
House
Diamond Ring
Stocks/Bonds
Beach House
House Hold furniture

4. Can liabilities be seen as good acquisitions? Circle Yes or No and explain why.

_____

_____

_____

_____

# Chapter V
## Understanding Debt

**Good Debt** - debt acquired from the purchase of assets (ex. mortgage, car note, student loans)

**Bad Debt** - debt acquired from the purchase of liabilities (ex. cash advance or title loans, credit card debt, high-interest loans)

# Assignment:

1. List your good debt

_____

_____

_____

_____

_____

_____

_____

_____

2. List your bad debt in the order of highest debt

_____

_____

_____

_____

_____

_____

_____

_____

3. What behavior(s) you must change to not incur more bad debt and future bad debt

_____

_____

_____

_____

_____

_____

## 4. Develop a plan to eliminate

_____
_____
_____
_____
_____
_____
_____
_____
_____

# Chapter VI
## Use money

*Priorities verses wants* – to determine the difference between priorities and wants. Priorities are those things that take precedent over your wants. Priorities categories are monthly bills (electricity, car note, mortgage, kids' necessities, etc...). On the other hand wants are what you desire but can live without or can put off until a later date. Sometimes mistakes are made when a want is categorized as a need. For example when I was in college I couldn't I didn't have the discretion income to have cable thus I opt out of the monthly expense of a cable bill. It is choices like such that you have to determine what is a priority verses a want.

*Planning and researching purchases* – to make a purchase on large items or costly items researching before purchasing is best. Take the time to compare quality and features of products so when you go to purchase you are less prone to fall for the typical sell pitch. For example if you need a washer and dryer research and compare the different brands, models, features and cost. Then make a decision according to your budget. In some cases you may not need all the features but something less expensive and practical but has the longevity and quality you'll need. Making purchasing of this nature your focus should be fulfilling the need according to your budget and a level of quality that will give you endurance. Sometimes you have to pay more for a greater quality but be assured that its longevity will pay off in the end. Don't always focus the cheapest brand if you can afford a better quality because quality will outlast the cheapest brand. In your planning plan ahead so you can give yourself a 3 to 4 month window if you can this will allow you to put money aside for a large purchase so when you have researched your products you'll be able to save and purchase it with cash. Always try to work towards cash payments and paying off within a short time period. This practice will enhance your credit viability and you'll become an owner. Take the wash and dry example after you have completed your research you can start to save money to make the purchase. Once you purchase the washer and dryer by paying cash then you feel a since of accomplishment and financial freedom as opposed to paying on the washer and dryer over several years. Most important if you follow this practice for large household products such as furniture, appliances, electronics (TV) you will own all these products and no monthly payments; what an accomplishment. This practice takes discipline and patience to have a house full of paid furniture and products.

Building perpetual wealth
Appendix

# Chapter VII
## Behavior Towards Money

*What you should do in your:*

**20's**
1. Develop healthy Financial Habits
2. Get out of credit card and college debt
3. Once your money is free, invest in
      a. 401k
      b. Other retirement plans
      c. Start a Roth IRA

**30's**
1. Contributing more to 401k and other retirement plans
2. Auto draft paychecks for retirement
3. Save the max
4. Don't worry about market volatility
5. Avoid taking on too much debt during your 30s so you will have enough cash to save for retirement

**40's**
1. Turbocharge your retirement saving during these years
2. See a financial planner who can act as a sounding board and help keep you on track and tweak your allocation mix
3. Coordinate with your spouse to save more
4. Put any raises and bonuses toward your retirement savings
5. Figure out how much you'll need to maintain your lifestyle in retirement

**50's**

1. Try to save as much as you can for the years you won't be able to save enough

2. Start thinking about when to you will start drawing social security

3. Reduce your expenses (downsize to save money)

4. Get in the habit of living on a fixed income and saving the extra money

5. This will help you get ready for managing your spending in retirement

# Chapter VIII
### Process to Perpetual Wealth

***Education/Career*** – to obtain a higher education degree to position yourself to have a career. There is a difference between a job and a career. Also to obtain a skill is important. It is always best to obtain either a skill or degree in a field that will give you a career. Selecting a degree field must be based upon your aptitude and ability. It not how much money you make it is how discipline you are with what you make. Some careers pay more than others so do not select a career based upon its financial gain but based upon your ability and passion. For example if you have a passion to be an educator (school teacher) as opposed to a computer programmer then become an educator because you'll be fulfilling your purpose and you'll have a since of satisfaction. Both careers will take discipline in managing the finances. Please review the Labor Bureau Statistics for educational attainment in the appendix as it indicates estimated earnings according to education levels.

***Process*** - the process of savings according to pods, ponds, lakes, streams and rivers. Saving is a necessity for financial stability and building wealth, don't be afraid to start small (i.e. $5.00 a week) and build from there and the goal is to work for money early so that money can eventually work for you in the future.

***-Pods*** – overflow or small emergency money, should be $300 to $500, used for unexpected bills or maintenance issues

***-Ponds*** – large scale emergency money, should be $1,000 to 3,000, used for major car breakdowns, unplanned medical bills, or planned house repairs

*-Lakes* – savings, should only have money going in (never being withdrawn), does not have to start with a lot of money, and a percentage of every pay check must be budgeted.

*-Streams* – investments, investments provide increase as they are appreciating assets that either provide a steady cash flow or builds on the invested funds, understand the risk versus reward for any investments being considered

*-Rivers* – retirement funds/IRAs/Pensions, they are mainly set up through employers, understand the long term projection of the fund (s) and how they match up with retirement plans.

Pods and Ponds are replenished every month (if not used, they are moved to lakes), wants should be acquired through petty cash (discretionary income) or planned for future, money for each category must be kept separately and not mingled and controls should be put in place to combat personal weaknesses and tendencies.

# HIERARCHY OF SAVING

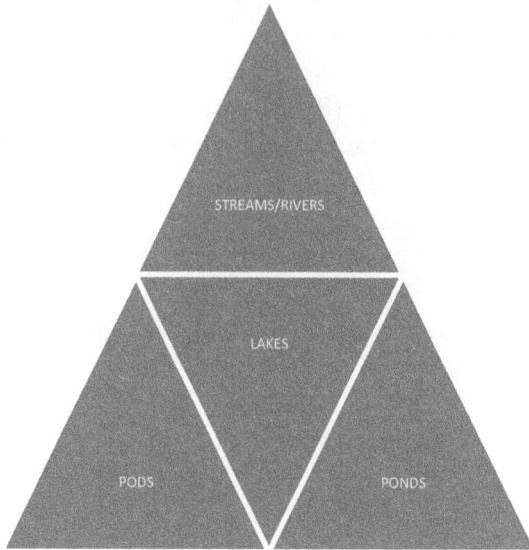

***Discipline*** – Webster's dictionary states that discipline is a way of behaving that shows a willingness to obey rules or orders, a rule or system of rules governing conduct or activity, having self-control. It is not a matter of how much money you earn it's the ability to discipline yourself to the plan you've set out. Any level of accomplishment it will take discipline to a pattern of behavior that will lead to success. Likewise the ability to exercise self-control in this area of your life can produce successful living.

# *Assignment:*

1. What is your educational attainment level? (Review the educational attainment chart in the appendix)

_____

_____

_____

_____

2. What is educational attainment level or skill you desire to achieve if you have not achieved it?

_____

_____

_____

_____

3. Which process do you currently use? (Circle)
a. Pods
b. Ponds
c. Lakes
d. Streams
e. Rivers

4. Which processes would you like to implement?
a. Pods
b. Ponds
c. Lakes
d. Streams
e. Rivers

# Chapter IX
How to get a strong financial infrastructure

Understand – is to understand where you are in your finances; at this point the keys are in your hands and you control your financial destiny.

Self- assessment
   a. Debts
   b. Bills
   c. Income
   d. Priorities (needs) not wants
   e. Credit Report and Score

Plan – according to Webster's definition a plan is a set of actions that have been thought of as a way to do or achieve something, something that a person intends to do. Once you determine and gather all the facts of where you stand with you finances then it's time to develop a plan. Before implementing your plan make sure you understand that requirements needed for success of the plan, remember that sacrifice will be required and that there are no short cuts. (assignment)
   a. Create a plan to where you plan to go, write it out as it serves as your vision
   b. Include all key stakeholders (spouse, children, etc.) in the plan and planning process
   c. Set realistic goals
   d. The plan becomes your ***contract*** once it's finalized

Process – the process for building a strong financial infrastructure is assessing your finances, set goals, create a plan, execute and achieve.

Work – work your plan behavior, discipline, review (assessment)

Repeat- to repeat the process that is laid out above in "c"

# Chapter X
## Financial Nuggets

***Emergency savings:*** We all need it. How to build it. Start today. - About one in three American families don't have any savings. Without savings, one emergency situation can push them over the financial brink.

    - Invest more money into your retirement funds to lower your tax bracket to save money.

    - Use 0% interest credit cards to transfer credit card debt to and pay it off

    - Look to cut down on monthly reoccurring expenses that will turn into long-term gains

    - Refinancing your mortgage to a lower rate allows for savings in the thousands over the life of the mortgage

    - Maximizing your credit score will allow you to receive lower interest loans that will save you money over the years

***Savings start-up strategies:*** Start small, keep it separate from spending money, make it automatic 50

(drafts or direct deposits), and unexpected money (tax refund or bonus) should go into savings.

- Emotions will take you down a dead-end road and leave you stranded.

- Remember, to achieve your financial goals, sacrifice will be required.

- Work for money early in life so that money can work for you later.

- Spontaneous spending is not a behavior that should ever be exercised.

- Wealth is not only for you but to be passed on to your children.

- Trying something new is uncomfortable, but trust the process.

- Equation for financial success = plan + process + discipline.

- You must change your behavior and habits to get a different result
- Emotion can never be your guide.

# Chapter XI
## Conclusion

What are you waiting to do later that you can actually do now? Many people often put off financial management until they get in a crisis and then they try to decide how to meet a financial crisis' need. If you make managing your personal finances a priority you will find that you can live in a level peace and harmony because you have a financial plan that prepares you for the unforeseen financial crisis. The key to managing your finance is discipline. You can accomplish a lot when you operate with a mind-set of strategy, delayed gratification, patience, and long term gain. Being willing to make sacrifices that are temporary for future gains is crucial as well. Many times people really fall short in this area because making a sacrifice means you have to give up something that you desire for the purpose of a futuristic goal. For example: if you desire to purchase a home you may sacrifice making other purchases at the time, such as a new car or if you desire to achieve a degree you may have to sacrifice and purchase a pre-owned vehicle as opposed to new vehicle. When you make a sacrifice it may look like you are forfeiting something but in essence you are just putting yourself in a better financial position to make the purchase because you have prepared by saving.

Another key element of managing your finances is to make good decisions. Make certain that your decisions will have a long term and positive impact for you. Don't make decisions based on your emotions but on data (facts) and trends. Emotions don't take in considerations all the elements of future situations. For example: if you are madly in love with a certain car but according to your financial plan/budget it is out of your price range purchasing the car is not a good decision. Emotionally you see yourself driving that car and you feel like you'll be seen and viewed a certain way. However, if it is out of your price range you should not proceed.

Timing is another key in successfully managing your finances. Your ability to patiently wait for a better time to purchase or wait until you have saved up for a purchase is a good practice. Many call this delayed gratification because you decide to put off a purchase for a later date and time. When you are waiting it's a good time to research the product so you'll know the 53 amount of money to save. Finally, the most important message is *start today managing your finances and you'll position yourself for a better tomorrow.*

# Appendix XII

Discipline. In Merriam-Webster Dictionary online. Retrieved from http://www.merriam-webster.com/dictionary/discipline

Frankel, M. (2016, January 2). 5 Ways to Save Thousands. *The Motley Fool*. Retrieved from http://www.fool.com/retirement/general/2016/01/02/5-ways-to-save-thousands-in-2016.aspx

Huang, J. (2016, January 5). Emergency Savings. *USA Today*. Retrieved from http://www.usatoday.com/story/money/personalfinance/2016/01/05/emergency-household-savings-spending/76277972/

MyFICO (2016) . (Graph illustrate how credit scores are calculated) Retrieved from http://www.myfico.com/crediteducation/whatsinyourscore.aspx

United States Department of Labor (2016). *Bureau of Labor Statistics*

(Employment Projection). Retrieved from http://www.bls.gov/emp/ep_chart_001.htm

United States Department of Labor. (2016) (Graph illustrates the earnings and unemployment rates by educational attainment). Retrieved from http://www.bls.gov/emp/ep_chart_001.htm

http://finance.yahoo.com/news/

http://www.msn.com/en-us/money

https://www.learnvest.com/lp/make-progress-in-new-year/

# FICO Score Calculation

**How a FICO Score breaks down**

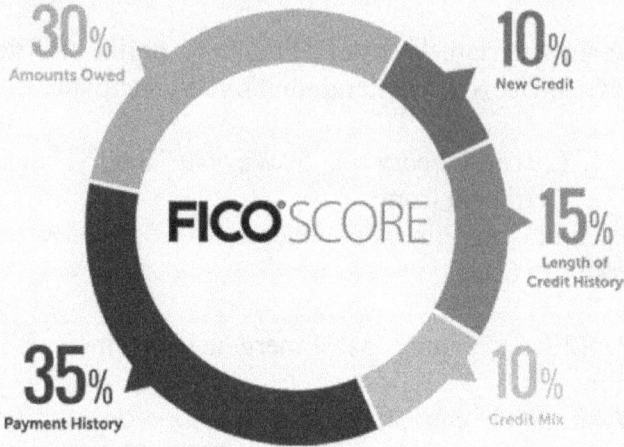

These percentages are based on the importance of the five categories for the general population. For particular groups—for example, people who have not been using credit long—the relative importance of these categories may be different.

### Labor Bureau Statistics for education attainment

**Earnings and unemployment rates by educational attainment**

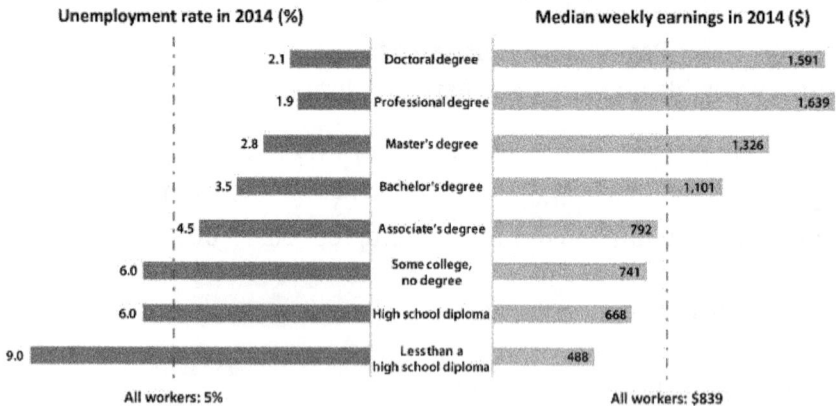

| Unemployment rate in 2014 (%) | | Median weekly earnings in 2014 ($) |
|---|---|---|
| 2.1 | Doctoral degree | 1,591 |
| 1.9 | Professional degree | 1,639 |
| 2.8 | Master's degree | 1,326 |
| 3.5 | Bachelor's degree | 1,101 |
| 4.5 | Associate's degree | 792 |
| 6.0 | Some college, no degree | 741 |
| 6.0 | High school diploma | 668 |
| 9.0 | Less than a high school diploma | 488 |
| **All workers: 5%** | | **All workers: $839** |

Note: Data are for persons age 25 and over. Earnings are for full-time wage and salary workers.
Source: Current Population Survey, U.S. Bureau of Labor Statistics, U.S. Department of Labor

## Data Table

Earnings and unemployment rates by educational attainment

| Earnings and unemployment rates by educational attainment | | |
| --- | --- | --- |
| Education attained | Unemployment rate in 2014 (Percent) | Median weekly earnings in 2014 |
| Doctoral degree | 2.1 | $1,591 |
| Professional degree | 1.9 | 1,639 |
| Master's degree | 2.8 | 1,326 |
| Bachelor's degree | 3.5 | 1,101 |
| Associate's degree | 4.5 | 792 |
| Some college, no degree | 6.0 | 741 |
| High school diploma | 6.0 | 668 |
| Less than a high school diploma | 9.0 | 488 |
| All workers | 5.0 | 839 |
| Note: Data are for persons age 25 and over. Earnings are for full-time wage and salary workers. Source: Current Population Survey, U.S. Department of Labor, U.S. Bureau of Labor Statistics | | |

# Household Financial Makeup

The Principle of PERPETUAL WEALTH

# The Principle of PERPETUAL WEALTH

| Family Budget Worksheet | | | |
|---|---|---|---|
| **Income** | **Budget** | **Actual** | **Difference** |
| Salary/wages | | | |
| Salary/wages | | | |
| | | | |
| | | | |
| | | | |
| **Total Income** | | | |
| **Deductions** | **Budget** | **Actual** | **Difference** |
| Tithes/offerings | | | |
| Savings (to set aside) | | | |
| Child Support, Alimony, etc. | | | |
| 401k | | | |
| IRA | | | |
| Donations | | | |
| Pocket Money | | | |
| Other | | | |
| **Total** | | | |

| Housing | Budget | Actual | Difference |
|---|---|---|---|
| Rent or Mortgage Payment | | | |
| Home Insurance & Taxes | | | |
| Home Repairs (to set aside) | | | |
| Utilities | | | |
| Phone - Home | | | |
| Phone - Cell | | | |
| Cable | | | |
| Water Bill | | | |
| Gas | | | |
| Electric Bill | | | |
| Furniture | | | |
| Other | | | |
| Other | | | |
| **Total** | | | |

| Debt Payment | Budget | Actual | Difference |
|---|---|---|---|
| Credit Card Payments | | | |
| Student Loan Payments | | | |
| Other | | | |
| Other | | | |
| Other | | | |
| **Total** | | | |
| **Food** | **Budget** | **Actual** | **Difference** |
| Groceries | | | |
| Eating Out | | | |
| Coffee & Bar | | | |
| Dining Out | | | |
| Lunch | | | |
| Other | | | |
| **Total** | | | |

| Transportation | Budget | Actual | Difference |
|---|---|---|---|
| Car Payment | | | |
| Car Insurance + Taxes | | | |
| Car Maintenance (to set aside) | | | |
| Gas | | | |
| Public Transit, Parking, Tolls | | | |
| Other | | | |
| **Total** | | | |
| **Family** | **Budget** | **Actual** | **Difference** |
| Day Care & Babysitting | | | |
| Activities & Lessons | | | |
| Allowances & Child Support | | | |
| Family Entertainment | | | |
| Memberships | | | |
| Events | | | |
| Music | | | |
| Other | | | |
| Other | | | |
| **Total** | | | |

| Personal & Health | Budget | Actual | Difference |
|---|---|---|---|
| Clothing | | | |
| Toiletries & Care Products | | | |
| Haircuts | | | |
| Gym & Sports Club Memberships | | | |
| Health, Life, & Disability Insurance | | | |
| Vision/Contacts | | | |
| Doctor & Dentist Visits | | | |
| Prescription & OTC Drugs | | | |
| Other | | | |
| **Total** | | | |
| **Education** | **Budget** | **Actual** | **Difference** |
| Tuition | | | |
| Books & Fees | | | |
| Supplies | | | |
| Other | | | |
| **Total** | | | |

| Entertainment | Budget | Actual | Difference |
|---|---|---|---|
| Tickets for Shows & Games | | | |
| Books & Magazine Subscriptions | | | |
| DVDs, CDs, Video Games | | | |
| Other | | | |
| **Total** | | | |
| **Miscellaneous** | **Budget** | **Actual** | **Difference** |
| Charity, Gifts, & Offerings | | | |
| Pet Supplies & Vet | | | |
| Entertaining Guests | | | |
| Pocket Money | | | |
| Other | | | |
| **Total** | | | |
| **Summary Calculation** | | | |
| Total Expenses | | | |
| | | | |
| Remaining Funds | | | |

# References XIII

http://www.bls.gov/emp/ep_chart_001.htm  - labor statistics

http://www.merriam-webster.com/dictionary/discipline - discipline
Webster's

http://www.myfico.com/crediteducation/whatsinyourscore.aspx -
FICO scores/report
USA today Financials articles

Learnvest.com

Money.msn

News.yahoo.com

YFmoneymailbag@yahoo.com

The Motley Fool

www.ingramcontent.com/pod-product-compliance
Lightning Source LLC
Chambersburg PA
CBHW031910200326
41597CB00012B/576